SEASONS

SEASONS

THOMAS LIM

WEE EDITIONS / SINGAPORE

To my mum and late father,
for giving me the strength
to be tough and to go against
your will, and pushing me
to be the best I can be.

To Jan, my partner, for keeping
me grounded, being my biggest
supporter and always standing
by my side.

Published in Singapore by Epigram Books
Wee Editions is an imprint of Epigram Books
www.epigrambooks.sg

Edited by Samantha Lee
Designed by Eng Chun Pang

Photo Credits: Matthew Tan p 12, 34—35,
37, 38—41, 42—43, 99, 106—107, front cover;
Derrick Lee p 2—3, 8, 20, 21, 30, 100, 102,
103, 104, 105; Alan Lee p 4—5, 6—7, 14—15,
16, 19, 22—29, 31—33, 45—49, 52—57, 62—65,
111, back cover; Edward Hendricks p 50—51,
58, 60—61, 66, 67; Frank Chen p 11, 71—97,
108, 109; Eng Chun Pang p 68—69

National Library Board, Singapore
Cataloguing-in-Publication Data

Lim, Thomas.
Seasons / Thomas Lim. —
Singapore : Wee Editions, 2014.
pages cm.

ISBN: 978-981-4615-79-2 (hardcover)
ISBN: 978-981-4615-78-5 (ebook)

1. Flower arrangement.   I. Title.

SB449
745.92 --dc23   OCN893826215

First Edition
10 9 8 7 6 5 4 3 2 1

CONTENTS

Dear Annie

Best wishes

Thomas Lim
2017

INTRODUCTION

y parents wanted me to be an engineer. They believed that the only way to achieve greatness was to become a professional in what were considered 'respectable fields'. But I had different plans for myself.

After graduating from high school, I worked for an interior design firm in Singapore. I fondly remember working on a project for a new condominium on Orchard Road. I was assigned the task of putting the final touches—of breathing life, romanticism and warmth—into a beautiful yet otherwise sterile room. I placed several green plants around the room, and arranged a simple centrepiece of roses and chrysanthemums on the dining room table. At that precise moment, I felt a wave of achievement, a sense that I had found my true calling in life. Everything lit up from that moment on.

I promptly quit my job at the interior design firm. For the next 30 years, my career would take me from my first flower shop near Orchard Road, to Hampshire in the UK, to California and to countless cities around the world in between.

I had found my true passion in floristry. In 1986, I took
The Society of Floristry (now absorbed into the British Florist
Association) examinations and graduated the following July.
In September, I entered the symposium competition and won
the title of Designer of the Year. In the same year, I created the
Bridal Bouquet of the Year. 1991, too, was a good year—I won the
Bouquet Innovation and Best Innovation Design competitions
in The Silk Show, Las Vegas.

After my forays in the international circuit, I finally returned to
Singapore in 1989, after my father's passing. I wanted to be near
my mother, and was happy to find myself once again surrounded
by my friends and family. I was featured as a homecoming hero
in Home and Decor Singapore magazine, and I became the first
Singaporean to be inducted into the American Institute of
Floral Designers.

When it comes to floral design and interior design, my major
inspirations come from nature and music. Finding beauty in
everyday settings fuels my creativity. I like to imagine Mozart
composing classical music in a grandiose, romantic setting.
I love to walk in the woods, absorbing the shapes, forms,
colours and sounds around me.

Two roads diverged in a wood, and I—
I took the one less travelled by,
         And that has made all the difference.

— *The Road Not Taken*, Robert Frost, 1916

In the same way summer melds into
the riotous colours and textures of autumn,
my career has been characterised
by gradual transitions.

Working in an industry so closely intertwined with the movement
of the earth around the sun, it is no wonder the influence of
passing seasons has weaved itself into my working life. In the
same way summer melds into the riotous colours and textures of
autumn, my career has been characterised by gradual transitions—
from Singapore to the UK and back to Singapore; from working
with fresh flowers to silk. The passing of seasons symbolises renewal
and growth; a beautiful and natural progression that, hopefully, is
captured in this book.

I hope this book inspires and encourages you to reach for the
stars and achieve your own perfection in flower arrangement.
To me, floral design is more than just a hobby, and with the
right encouragement, you can also achieve a long and beautiful
career as a professional floral designer. Just remember to strive
to be unpredictable, interesting, innovative and different.

With that, I present to you: a culmination of 30 years of
professional floral design.

Thomas Lim

FRESH AS SPRING

I often gave discarded flowers
a second chance, using their bits and pieces
to make beautiful arrangements,
bouquets and centrepieces.

t was 1982. At the tender age of 21, after quitting my job at an interior design firm, I opened the doors to Autumn Florist— my first flower shop in Ming Arcade, near Orchard Road. Though business was booming, I felt stunted by the lack of professional training in Singapore's floral design scene. Then, in 1983, I met Rona Coleman, an experienced and talented floristry teacher from Gloucestershire. Along with her husband Stanley, she has been an invaluable mentor who has always encouraged me to live up to my full potential. With their help, I continued my studies in English Floristry at the Society of Floristry (now absorbed into the British Florist Association) while working part-time at M&J Stevens, a flower shop in Hampshire.

I remember my time there fondly—the owners, June and Dave
Evans, became my adopted English parents. They soon gave me
full rein of the shop, and I often gave discarded flowers a second
chance, using their bits and pieces to make beautiful arrangements,
bouquets and centrepieces. I loved decorating the shop windows—
often surprising residents of the small village. They'd stop and
exclaim, "That bloody Asian boy has done it again!"

One of my fondest memories to date was the opportunity in 1988
to design a bouquet for the late Princess Diana, who was attending
the opening of a new children's hospital in Hampshire. A pair of
twin girls were to present her with the bouquet, so I created two
half-bouquets to come together as one. In the absence of foliage
I created ribbon tubes to form leaf-like shapes, but everything
else was fresh. I still remember the sweet aroma of cream and
champagne roses, tuberoses, freesias and alstroemerias.

LEFT

An arrangement of leftover
florals from the design
room, combined with berry
vines, rose hips and petals,
and eucalyptus leaves.
The twig cover, bound
with moss and hydrangeas,
is the focal point, while
tulips breathe life to the
entire composition.

RIGHT

This irregularly-shaped
porcelain vase is set with
a base of moss, anthurium
and celosia, allowing the
painted wooden bird
to sing along with the
hyacinth and berries.

OVERLEAF, LEFT
Visual merchandising
display of a springtime
floral arch.

OVERLEAF, RIGHT
The white phalaenopsis
orchid represents pure,
distilled elegance. Here,
kiwi vine is twined to
create the illusion of
natural movement.

LEFT
A three-piece geometric
design set of snake grass
and Vanda orchids.

RIGHT
Vanda orchids arranged
in this Versace vase give a
simultaneously modern and
classic accent to the room.

LEFT
A linear display with
a simple bunch of
cattail leaves and irises
in a glass vase.

ABOVE, LEFT
Blue irises with a mini
rose spray and peonies
tucked in with eucalyptus
and cattle leaves.

ABOVE, RIGHT
Snake grass, intertwined
around blue irises.

LEFT
Mixed Victorian roses in
a contemporary glass bowl.

RIGHT
Magnolia branches simply
arranged in a glass cylinder.

PREVIOUS PAGE, LEFT
An intricate tropical
arrangement consisting
of mini heliconias, spider
orchids, lotus pods, mixed
greenery and vines.

PREVIOUS PAGE, RIGHT
Cattleya orchids with
moss, potted in a glass
vase accompanied by two
simple bunches of lilies.
These form a perfect trio.

LEFT
A bright and cheerful
arrangement of
freesias, ranunculus,
hydrangeas and ixora.

RIGHT
This centrepiece, arranged
with bunches of hydrangeas,
lilies and roses, is perfect
for a romantic occasion.

PREVIOUS PAGE, LEFT
A container, simply made
by binding bunches of
cattail leaves, accented
with a spray of asparagus
sprengeri, berries and
gloriosa lily.

PREVIOUS PAGE, RIGHT
An effortless greenery
arrangement in a crystal
vase, with snake grass,
peacock leaves and galax
leaves accented by
white anemones.

ABOVE

A windswept design formed
by a bloom broom arching
over a moss-covered dome,
with seed pods and a
snowball at the base.

ETERNAL SUMMER

RIGHT

An oxblood urn with a
cluster of ranunculus,
succulents and hydrangeas
entwined in grape vines.

The business of artificial flowers is booming; exploding in the last few decades into a multi-billion dollar industry. Modern silk and artificial flowers mirror live blooms so closely that it is difficult to tell the difference without a very close look. They have quite the long history, beginning over 1,500 years ago when ladies of the Imperial Palace in China wore them in their hair. In the 12th century, the Italians were the first to bring artificial flower arrangements to market, and by the 15th century, the French had mastered the art of making them, surpassing the Italians and eventually introducing the art form to America and the rest of the world. By the 1920s, florists had begun using artificial flowers to augment natural arrangements or as substitutes when certain flower types were unavailable, expensive or impractical.

You cannot simply throw
artificial flowers in a vase;
it takes a special touch
to make them look real.

In 1988, Creative Marketing Concepts (CMC) officially
invited me to their Cleveland, Ohio headquarters a week after
the American Institute of Floral Designers (AIFD) Symposium,
challenging me to design three silk flower arrangements.

This caught my attention—I noted that artificial flowers had the
benefit of prolonged beauty, and with some adjustments, could
be made better and more realistic in order to pique the interest
of future generations of floral designers. With both my formal
training in horticulture and experience in floral design, I became
integrally involved in the silk flower industry and have worked
closely with several artificial flower makers and designers to date.

Dedication, creativity and botanical knowledge are absolutely essential to the development of artificial flower prototypes. The process in which a single stem is produced can be a laborious and extensive experience—mould making, applying new colouring techniques, fabric selection, hand shaping and hand gluing, matching components, leaf stemming and assembly. Sometimes, it could be a day or two before a single complete silk flower is born. Yet despite the hard work, I relish the challenge of making artificial flowers flow naturally and realistically. You cannot simply throw artificial flowers in a vase; it takes a special touch to make them look real. The way they fall, the way they bend, the way they are arranged—all this makes a significant impact in elevating the arrangement to the realm of art.

I have been working with silk flowers for more than two decades. I love that I can use silk florals to create permanent art that can survive all temperatures. I love that they're easier to handle than fresh flowers. And I love that I need not depend on seasonal flowers to create beautiful arrangements. Now, summer lasts all year long.

RIGHT
A classic topiary in white: anemones, roses, ranunculus, snowballs, phalaenopsis and berries arranged in a porcelain urn.

PREVIOUS PAGE
A honey and cream
interior setting,
accented with
champagne roses.

ABOVE
A contemporary
arrangement of red
amaryllis, interlocked
with pear branches and
monstera leaves.

RIGHT
A dome-shaped design
with varieties of silk roses,
ranunculus, snowballs,
lisanthus and sweet peas in
a handmade ceramic pot.

LEFT
Pear branches determine
the outline of this
table arrangement.
The combination of
blue and white creates
a calm atmosphere.

RIGHT
A simple Vanda orchid
plant, the pot itself
overflowing with
abundant roots.

OVERLEAF
Parisian roses, lilacs,
anemones, Queen
Anne's lace and ivy
arranged horizontally
in this Venetian glass
vase result in a
romantic display.

LEFT
Silk cymbidium orchids
arranged in a mossed glass
vase add a permanent
accent to this bathroom.

OVERLEAF
Cranberry-red accents
create an interesting
contrast between interior
and exterior in this
Sentosa bungalow.

ABOVE
The uplifted horizontal
design playfully extends
the lilac flowers away from
the vase. Birch branches
that sprint and twist above
add a touch of whimsy.

RIGHT
The green Sarracenia
that extends upwards
is complemented by a
harmony of textures:
soft white phalaenopsis
orchids, curly willows that
reach into the air, and
the depth of amaryllis.

Branches and kiwi vines create flow of movement. These are paired with the gathering of ranunculus, hydrangeas, scabiosas, alliums and rose hips in a rounded shape at the base. A ceramic mouse created by French sculpture artist Valerie Courtet adds a touch of playfulness.

This arrangement appears ready for flight. Monstera leaves extend, wing-like, over the vase as amaryllis rises to form a strong central spine. Spirea and orchid buds add an ethereal accent to the vertical lines. A large succulent rests atop a soft bedding of hydrangeas and snowballs, like a beating heart.

BELOW

A master bedroom in a
cream and taupe palette,
simply accented with
blue sweet pea flowers.

RIGHT

A joyous, buoyant pair of
arrangements incorporates
poppies and passiflora,
which appear to dance
across the table.

An Autumn Wedding

In 1987, I moved to northern California following my time in the United Kingdom. There, I met Fei Fei Shen, who introduced me to the silk flower industry and is one of my dearest friends today. Fei is an accomplished artist and then owned a silk flower warehouse. She introduced me to other permanent floral wholesalers, and I began teaching florists in the United States the art of creating refined wedding bouquets.

Fei invited me into her home with open arms, and I became godfather to her two daughters, Nikki and Jessica. In the fall of 2012, I had the immense pleasure of creating the floral arrangements for Nikki's wedding. It was held in the Four Seasons Hotel in Hangzhou, China, in a beautiful classical Chinese garden. We decided on a beautiful, rich palette that would match the opulence of the ballroom and the classic beauty of the garden. We choose different shades of purples, pinks, golds and white. For both the garden ceremony and the evening banquet, I weaved silk flowers in with fresh, for the simple reason that not all the varieties I desired were in season. Snowball-like green hydrangeas, the purple-and-pink tones of clematis and delicate blue lilacs enlivened the garden under the placid autumn sunlight, while a hint of glamour gilded dinner proceedings. Each table had its own customised centerpiece bouquet. Silk flowers such as handmade mini rose balls, purple delphiniums and pink lisianthus nestled amongst the lush vibrancy of fresh curly willows, asparagus ferns, Vanda orchids and cabbage roses. Handmade silk butterflies, perched on the branches, and clusters of fresh strawberries and grapes added the final Dionysian touch.

Of the hundreds of weddings I have worked on in the past 30 years, this was by far the most memorable.

Nikki's wedding colours
were a combination of
shades of purple, pink and
gold. The ceremony's decor
matched the aura of the fall
garden—light, airy, rich
colour tones celebrating
fall season at its best.

LEFT

A romantic arrangement
in silk comprising
ranunculus, passiflora,
clementis, hydrangeas and
snowballs. This was set
beautifully on the coffee
table in the bridal suite.

RIGHT

Putting the final touches
on the floral arrangements.

A grouping of green
cymbidiums, mini dianthus
and calla lilies, accented
with dracaena and wrapped
with monstera leaves,
exudes a classic formality.

A vertical arrangement
consisting of snake grass,
beargrass and white roses.

LEFT
Pink cymbidium orchids
and snowballs dance
around curly willows,
imparting elegance to the
lobby of the bridal suite.

RIGHT
Flower girls were decked out
in the palette of champagne
and cream, accented with
subtle hints of purple.

ABOVE

A posy of pink bourbon
roses, the bride's
favourite colour.

RIGHT

The bridesmaids had
hair pieces with fresh
gerberas, sweet Williams
and amaranthus to match
the beauty of the garden.

LEFT
While the decor at the ceremony was whimsical and free flowing, the bridal bouquets were uniform and traditional. The bridesmaids carried bourbon roses, and the bride carried a large bouquet of white roses in a pomander shape.

OVERLEAF
Preparing for the ceremony was quite the experience. It had been raining for the past three days, and the weather forecasted rain. We were all prepared for the worst. But on the morning of the wedding day, the skies cleared and the sun emerged. It was a perfect autumn day in Hangzhou.

This topiary consists of
fresh dianthus, Vanda
orchids and roses.
To achieve the harmony
of colours, silk clematis,
snowballs and ranunculus
were mixed in with the
fresh flowers, since these
were not available during
the autumn season.

BELOW
Hanging crystals
represented dew drops,
while woolly ribbon
bows softened the
arrangement. A Vanda
orchid, captured in glass,
added a touch of glamour
to the surroundings.

PREVIOUS PAGE
Nikki and Chris Cannon
taking their vows in the
Chinese garden at the Four
Seasons Hotel, Hangzhou.

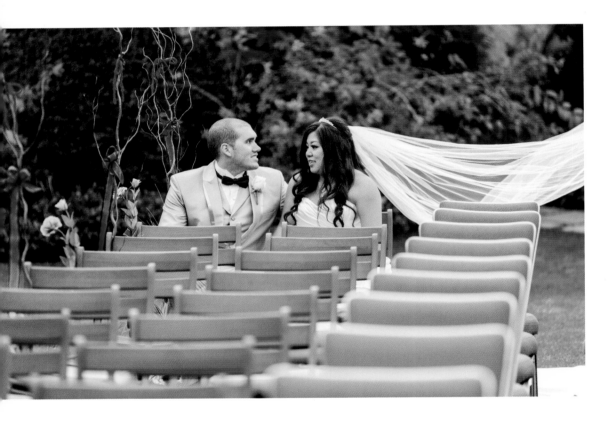

LEFT
The newlyweds sharing
a quiet moment.

RIGHT
Floral hair pieces and
bouquets related the
bridesmaids' outfits
to their surroundings.

PREVIOUS PAGE
Pink matiola and
green snowballs dance
around curly willows.

ABOVE
Nikki's sister, Jessica,
took three days to make
the three-tiered wedding
cake. A true labour of love,
each tier was a different
flavour and was spread with
butter cream; the magnolia
blooms were made with
gum paste and sugar.

RIGHT
The fresh and silk flower
combination in this
topiary rises harmoniously
above the banquet table.
The braided coloured
ribbons represent the
joining of two families and
cultures, the intertwining
of east and west.

FESTIVE
FLORALS

RIGHT

This handmade wired
reindeer in gold glitter
sets the focal point for this
tall centrepiece, accented
with hand-wrapped
green poinsettias and
glass ball ornaments.

Passersby are often drawn to the shop windows at my showroom, At Home and Garden. Transforming the window displays on a regular basis has become my forte, the spacious double shop front providing ample room for the flowers. Each year, I invest particular effort in four major displays, which are eagerly awaited by our regulars: Spring, Summer, Christmas and Chinese New Year. In fact, shopfront presentation is the best way to promote designs and products—in all the 10 years my shop has been open, I have not spent a single cent on advertising.

LEFT

A pair of recycled Prosecco
bottles provides elegant
containers for this festive
arrangement. The red
beaded wire trumpet is
hand-woven and twirls
around the gold grass.

There are so many shades
to play with: scarlet, ruby,
maroon, burgundy…
the possibilities are limitless.

One of the perennially popular festive colours is red. To some,
the red rose is associated with love, while in Chinese culture the
colour corresponds with fire and symbolises joy and good fortune.
Red is also a traditionally Christmas colour, persisting in nature
even when temperatures plummet. Think of the bright red holly
berries, and the shock of the robin's red breast in the snow.
There are so many shades to play with: scarlet, maroon, ruby,
burgundy… the possibilities are limitless. Here is a selected array
of my festive pieces created for large-scale floral events, costumes
and personal celebrations.

BELOW

A simple centrepiece
arrayed on a leather
tray, with handmade
velvet poinsettias, holly
leaves and a snowball.

RIGHT

A traditional festive
ambience is evoked by
this table arrangement,
which consists of red ilex
berries, velvet poinsettias
and holly leaves.

PREVIOUS PAGE
In this formal living
room in a contemporary
bungalow in Singapore,
the white hourglass vase
on the side table, spilling
over with coral tree flowers,
softens the atmosphere.
An oversized silk floral
centrepiece with fuchsia
peonies, red roses and
crabapples adds a festive
touch on the coloured
glass coffee table.

LEFT
Gold silk poinsettias
with a mixed seed pod
spray arranged in a
contemporary 'twin' design.

RIGHT
One of our most popular
traditional festive
arrangements comprises
velvet poinsettias, red
berries, gold gilded
leaves and seed pods.

LEFT

A crescent-shaped
arrangement of silk
peonies, zinneas, snowballs
and quince blossoms makes
this the perfect Chinese
New Year decoration.

ABOVE

Jenny Chia is a dear
friend and muse. This
party costume in red and
gold comprises three
types of ribbons woven
through a wire frame,
formed to drape over her
shoulder. A flower-laden
choke and hairpiece
complete the outfit.

ACKNOWLEDGEMENTS

In celebrating a successful 30-year floristry career, I'd like to thank all the people I have met from all over the world and all walks of life; who have supported me so greatly in my journey as a professional floral designer. Without you, I would not be where I am today. The contemporary bouquets presented in this book represent my history and relationship with each and every one of you, and I hope you will accept it as a token of my gratitude.

A big thank you to June and Dave Evans for giving me the opportunity to work in their flower shop in Portchester, Hampshire from 1984 to 1988. I gained a tremendous amount of experience working there.

Many thanks to Fei Fei for getting me started with my first design show in California, and many more shows that followed throughout the USA and Canada between 1988 and 1992. I am grateful for her hospitality, through which I got to know her lovely daughters Nikki and Jessica.

Nikki, thank you for your great help with the book, and for being the flower girl in some of my shows in the '90s.

Thanks to Jay Houston for introducing me to the permanent flower industry in 1988.

My sincere thanks to my three sisters, See See, Chui Chui
and Kiam Kiam for always giving me a helping hand in
times of stress.

Thanks to my brother Jeffery and my sister-in-law Susan for
being there for me since the beginning of my floristry journey.

Thanks to Irene Lim for all her support and for assisting me
at the showroom.

Thanks to Eric Smith for help with the book.

Thanks to Frank Chen and his team of photographers,
who took such wonderful pictures of Nikki's wedding.

Thanks to Alan Lee, Edward Hendricks, Matthew Tan and
Derrick Lee, who did most of the photography for this book.

Many thanks to Sophie Kho, editor of Home and Decor
Singapore magazine for featuring many of my creations.

Big thank you to the creative team at Epigram Books for
making my dreams come true.

Please visit www.athomeandgarden.com.sg for more pictures
of my work.